TRAINS AND TOW BOATS

By Bill Trombello
Illustrated by Nick Tangen

Copyright ©2013

TECHNICAL TRAINING CONSULTANTS INC.

TRAINS AND TOW BOATS

Copyright ©2013

Library of Congress Cataloging-in-Publication Data
Trombello, William,
Trains and Tow Boats/ William Trombello
ISBN: 978-0-9842998-1-2   Juvenile
Copyright Registered: 2013
First Published by Technical Training Consultants Inc. in the USA
801 Warrenville Rd.
Suite 222
Lisle, IL 60532
www.ttc-train.com
May, 2013

TRAINS AND TOW BOATS

"Engineer Obie, please report to my Office."

"Good morning Jim."

"Obie, I have some exciting news. The Willow Falls Railroad has just acquired Midwestern Towing, a towboat company."

"Jim, we run a railroad, why do we need a towboat company?"

"Obie, trucking is the most expensive way to transport anything. Our freight trains can move a ton of freight 484 miles on a single gallon of fuel. That's four times more efficient than trucking. However, the most cost-efficient method of transporting goods is by water, not rail. Now we can use towboats to transport coal to the power plant, and grain to New Orleans.

Obie and Mike decided to see for themselves. They went to the rail yard and got into their trusty GP38 locomotive. They coupled 15 carloads of coal to the train, and pulled all of the cars to the river depot, where coal is unloaded and loaded on river barges.

"Welcome aboard, I've been expecting you. My name is Joe, and I'm the towboat's chief engineer. I hope you won't mind waiting for me in the engine room, while I put diesel fuel into my boat. I'm the P. I. C., and fueling the vessel requires all of my attention."

"What's the P. I. C?" Obie asks.

"P. I. C., is the person in charge, I have to make sure fueling the boat is done safely, and carefully. Obie, did you know that if a careless mechanic were to spill as little as one quart of oil into a river or lake, that quart of oil would produce an oil slick 2 acres in size?"

"Wow, I didn't know that" Obie exclaimed. "Carry on Joe! Mike and I will wait for you in the engine room."

In the engine room, Mike was surprised. "Look Obie, they use the same diesel engines we use in our locomotives."

Joe walked in. "Mike, you have good eyes! We use 2 diesel engines in this boat, and unlike your locomotive engine that turns a generator, our engines turn a marine gear connected to a propeller, which we call a 'wheel.' One of our diesel engines turns the propeller clockwise, and the other diesel engine turns the propeller counter clockwise. When both 'wheels' turn in opposite directions, the boat moves in a straight line through the water."

"Where do you put oil, or fuel filters into this engine?" asked Mike.

"We Don't!" Joe replied. "We use a special filterless system. We don't have to worry about disposing of dirty filters, or their boxes; we don't have to worry about oil that usually spills when filters are changed. This boat is one of the cleanest on the river! In fact, because our engines also have the latest emissions equipment, our boat never emits ugly black smoke, as other boats do."

Joe, Obie and Mike walked into the boat's galley.

"Joe, is this the kitchen?" Obie asked.

"On a boat the kitchen is called the galley," replied Joe. "Would you like to say hello to our cook Catherine? She's preparing her famous catfish fry for lunch."

The three men walked upstairs to the pilot's house. In this room, the boat captain steers the tow boat down the river.

"Captain Dickey, I would like to introduce you to engineer Obie and mechanic Mike from our railroad division," Joe said.

Captain Dickey decided to test Obie and Mike.

"Boys, would you like to take the wheel?" asked Captain Dickey. "Compared to driving a train down two tracks, I think you'll find it challenging to steer a towboat as it pushes all of these barges around bridges and piers!"

"We'll be happy to steer," said Obie. "But only if you take the controls of our locomotive pulling a 15 million pound, mile long train up and down hills!"

Everyone laughed. But Obie realized it's HARD to steer a towboat pushing barges.

"Captain Dickey, how do you connect all of those barges together?" Obie asks.

Captain Dickey answered, "Deck hands use big wire cables to tie the barges together. Rope is not strong enough. If one of those barges breaks away from our tow, it could crash into a bridge or pier, or even another boat!"

"By the way Obie, see that barge with the railroad tracks mounted on it?" Captain Dickey continued. "That barge will bring your new locomotive back to Willow Falls."

Obie smiled.

Obie now understood that tow boat workers have important skills and responsibilities. He asked, "Joe, how does a person become a chief engineer like you or a boat captain like Dickey?"

"I went to the Maritime Academy, where I received my engineering license. Dickey worked his way from deck hand to tow boat pilot to captain of the boat. You can't learn everything at school; experience also matters!"

The roar of the diesel engines sprang to life as the massive tow boat pulled away from the boat dock, and moved down the mighty river.

Mike then said, "Joe, Obie and I normally work eight hours a day. How long do you work?"

"Working on a towboat is different," Joe replied. "For twenty-eight straight days I work on the boat for twelve hours every day, then I get to go home for twenty eight days. We call it 28 on, and 28 off."

It was time for lunch. As Captain Dickey carefully drove the massive boat down the river, Joe, Mike and Obie enjoyed Catherine's wonderful fried catfish.

"When will Captain Dickey eat lunch?" Obie asks.

"As soon as the pilot relieves him." Joe replied.

"What's a pilot?"

"A pilot also knows how to drive a boat. He goes to school and earns a license to prove he is a certified boat driver."

Joe heard someone calling his name.

To Obie and Mike, Joe said, "For a few minutes, I need to leave you and watch my assistant engineer grease some fittings on the boat deck. We have a buddy system on our boat. Whenever we perform maintenance on the boat deck, someone always watches to be sure the working man doesn't fall into the water. Working on a towboat deck is just like swimming; you should never do it alone."

The massive towboat approached its final destination, the West Virginia coal dock.

"Obie, there's your new locomotive. Isn't it a beauty?" Joe said.

"Sure is" Obie replied.

With the massive tow boat docked, Obie and Mike start inspecting the GP20D locomotive. All locomotives are required to be thoroughly inspected every day.

"Hey Obie, take a look at this Caterpillar engine!" Mike cried. "This engine has 2100 horsepower, is whisper quiet, and is equipped with all the latest emissions modifications. It can really pull train cars, but you don't have to cover your ears or your nose as it runs."

"Mike and Obie then jumped into the cab. In the cab a train engineer can see down the tracks as he drives the train.

"This is just like looking from the top of a lighthouse" Mike exclaimed." "You can see everything around you."

Obie loved the locomotive. But he thought the company could make one improvement. He said "The locomotive is both quiet and clean. But let's talk to Jim about making the GP20D even cleaner. If we install a filterless system like the system on the tow boat, then we never have to worry about spilling oil. Then our locomotive will be really clean-or, as people say- it'll be clean and green."

Mike noticed something strange under the front draft pocket of the locomotive. It was a radar unit, which he thought was used to tell how fast the locomotive was moving.

 Obie explained that just like car wheels can slip on roads, train wheels can slip on train tracks. To help control the train, the locomotive has a "wheel creep system." Obie said, "When a wheel slips on this locomotive, the computer working with the radar lets the wheels slip just a little. When the wheels slip just a little, they create friction. Friction helps the wheels grab the tracks 40% better when the rails are slippery."

The tow boat was almost ready to go. Workers had loaded coal on some barges. A crane carefully lifted the GP20D locomotive and also put it on a barge.

As the massive towboat pushed the barges up river, Obie realized that towboats can transport almost anything, even truck trailers!

Obie asked, "Joe, what if we were to use barges to move truck trailers? It would be a whole lot cheaper to use barges to move truck trailers over long distances than trains or trucks."

The towboat arrived and docked at the river depot, The crane carefully unloaded the GP20D locomotive, and placed it on the railroad tracks.

Obie carefully backs up the GP20D, and, with a thunderous thunk, couples the new locomotive to twenty waiting coal cars.

Nest stop: the Willow Falls power plant!

The GP20D locomotive leaves the depot, wheels screeching on the rail, the wheel creep system helps the locomotive pull the heavy coal cars.

"Listen to the screeching of those wheel!" Obie shouts.

"Pull baby pull" Mike cheered.

As the train approached Salt Lick Curve, Obie wondered if the locomotive could pull the heavy cars around the curve and up the steep hill. He turned to Mike and said, "Now we'll see how special this wheel creep system is!"

The locomotive approached Salt Lick curve at 40 miles per hour. As the locomotive struggles up the elevated curve, its speed drops....... 30 miles per hour, 20 miles per hour, 10 miles per hour.

"Are we going to make it?" Obie shouts. "Our display screen is reporting that our motors are getting hot and our traction is decreasing! But I think this great locomotive can do it!"

Obie was right. With the wheels screeching, the train slowly reaches the top of Salt Lick Curve.

Obie celebrated.

"With our old GP38 locomotive, we normally pull fifteen coal cars up Salt Lick Curve. Today we pulled twenty cars up the curve. Our wheel creep system is amazing!"

The trip is only half over. Now, Obie and Mike take the train down hill to Willow Falls.

"We'll use the dynamic brake system," Obie told Mike. "Dynamic brake will slow the train down. It does this by changing the motors to generators."

Finally, the train arrives at the Willow Falls Power Plant. Mike and Obie unload the train cars and head for home

At the rail yard Big Jim welcome the two men home.

"What did you two think of our new towboat and new locomotive?" asked Jim.

Obie and Mike gave a big "thumbs up."

"Great," Jim replied. "I can't wait to hear about your trip. Let's talk over lunch. I'm buying."

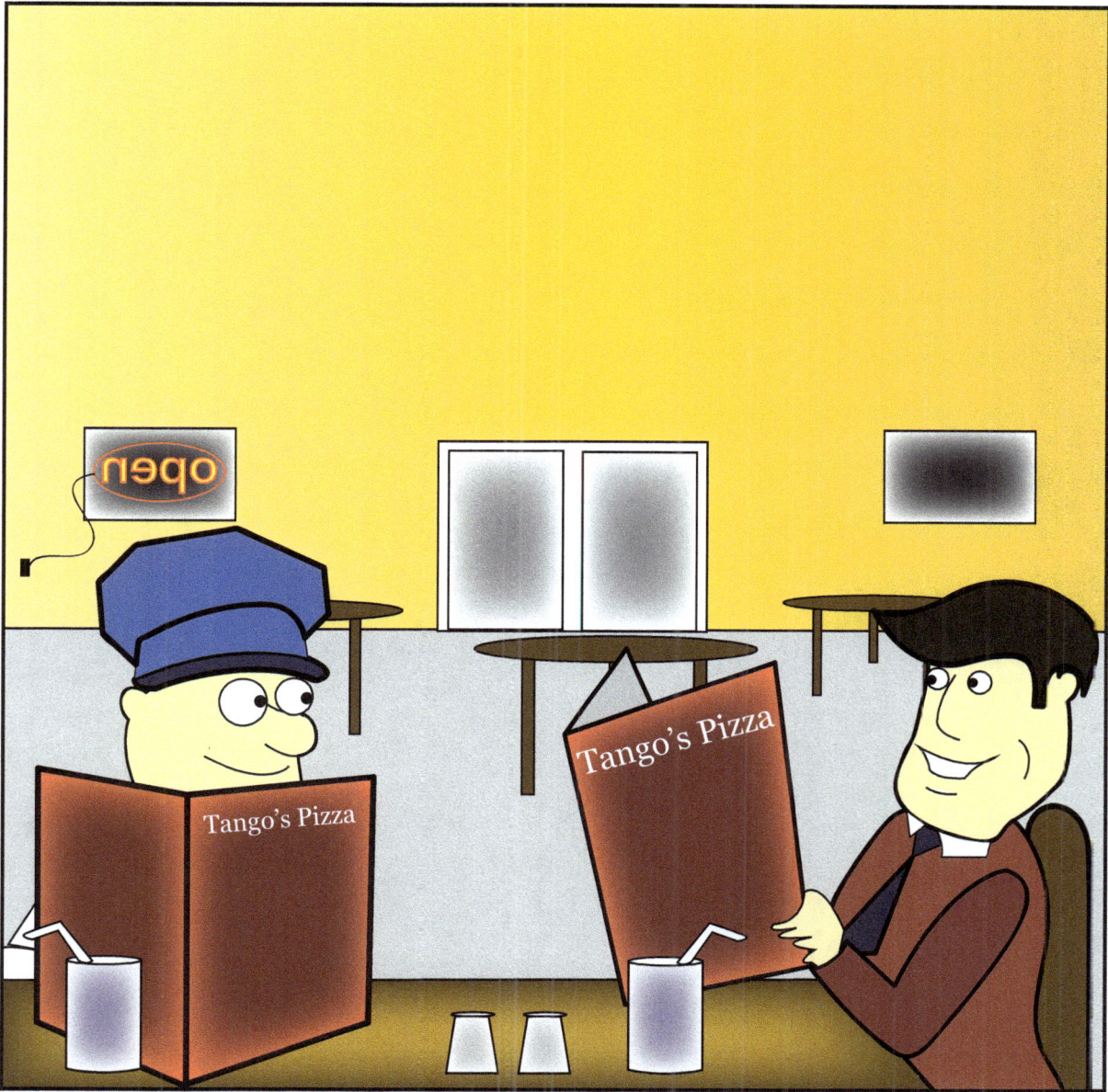

At lunch, Obie wondered about Jim's future plans.

"We now own both a freight railroad and a towboat company. What's next, Jim?" he asked.

Jim grinned.

"We use the Christmas train - our old E9 - only once every year. What if we used it to carry weekend passengers to Door County? People could have a holiday...............every week of the year!"

To be continued.............

Also by William Trombello

How a Real Locomotive Works
Trains and Real Locomotives
The Willow Falls Christmas Train

www.ingramcontent.com/pod-product-compliance
Lightning Source LLC
LaVergne TN
LVHW081326060426
835511LV00011B/1888